The Shakespeare Library

Shakespeare: A Life

WENDY GREENHILL
HEAD OF EDUCATION,
ROYAL SHAKESPEARE COMPANY
and
PAUL WIGNALL

Heinemann Library
Chicago, Illinois

Designed by Green Door Design
Printed in Hong Kong

04 03 02 01 00
10 9 8 7 6 5 4 3 2 1

Library of Congress Cataloging-in-Publication Data
Greenhill, Wendy, 1949-
    Shakespeare: a life / Wendy Greenhill and Paul Wignall.
        p. cm. – (The Shakespeare library)
    Includes bibliographical references (p.) and index.
    Summary: The life and times of a professional actor, businessman, and playright
who was born in Stratford-upon-Avon and whose plays are still performed and valued for
their insights into human nature.
    ISBN 1-57572-287-9 (lib. bdg.)
    1. Shakespeare, William, 1564-1616—Juvenile literature. 2. Dramatists,
English—Early modern, 1500-1700—Biography—Juvenile literature. [1. Shakespeare,
William, 1564-1616. 2. Dramatists, English.] I. Wignall, Paul. II. Title.
PR2895.G74 2000
822.3'3—dc21
[B]
                                                                99-055122

Acknowledgments
The authors and publishers would like to thank the following for permission to use
photographs and other illustrative material:

Berkeley Castle, Gloucestershire, p. 20; The Bridgeman Art Library, p. 19, 23; The Bodleian Library, p. 14;
The British Library, pp. 16, 21; Fotomas Index, p. 9; The National Portrait Gallery, pp. 17, 25;
The Public Records Office, p. 28; The Royal Shakespeare Company, p. 27; The Shakespeare Centre Library: Stratford-upon-Avon, pp. 4, 5, 6, 7, 8, 12, 13, 15, 26, 29, 31; The Victoria and Albert Museum, p. 11.

Every effort has been made to contact copyright holders of any material reproduced in this book. Any omissions will be rectified in subsequent printings if notice is given to the publisher.

Some words are shown in bold, **like this.** You can find out what they mean by looking in the glossary.

CONTENTS

STRATFORD, 1564

William Shakespeare was a professional actor, a businessman, and a playwright. Today, nearly 400 years after his death, his plays are still performed, moving audiences to tears and to laughter. Shakespeare's works tell us much about **Elizabethan** England. What is most remarkable is that Shakespeare's plays can still tell us something about ourselves.

SHAKESPEARE'S BIRTHPLACE

Stratford-upon-Avon is one of the most famous tourist attractions in the world. Every year, hundreds of thousands of people come to see the house where Shakespeare was born, the garden of the house where he died, and the church where he is buried. Visitors can also see his plays performed in one of the Royal Shakespeare Company's three theaters. Today's Stratford has many shops, parking lots, and cafés. Yet there is still something of Shakespeare's town as it was during his lifetime. The street

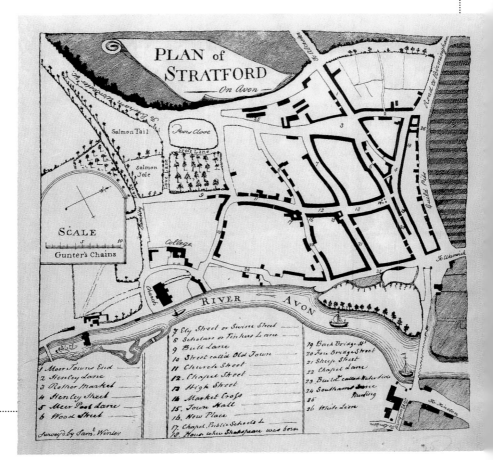

This map shows Stratford-upon-Avon in 1759.

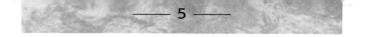

patterns remain much the same. There are still buildings in the town that he would have known. Even the busy atmosphere is not new. In 1564, Stratford-upon-Avon was a busy market town and an important river crossing for the people who traveled between England's Midlands and the city of London.

SHAKESPEARE'S FAMILY

William's father, John Shakespeare, came to Stratford in 1551 or 1552. He lived in a house on Henley Street. His family was from Snitterfield, a village just north of Stratford. The records of court hearings at that time show that on April 29, 1552, he was fined for having a rubbish heap near his house. John Shakespeare was a glover and whittawer, which is a person who works with white leather. It was a skilled trade for which he would have worked first as an apprentice. He may have apprenticed for a Stratford glover named Thomas Dickson before opening a shop of his own. He was obviously successful, because, in 1556, he bought the house next door to his on Henley Street. He linked the two houses to make one big house, which is now known as William Shakespeare's Birthplace. Stratford was an up-and-coming town, and John Shakespeare was not going to be left behind.

John Shakespeare married in 1557 or early 1558. His wife was Mary Arden, the youngest of eight daughters of Robert Arden. They lived in Wilmcote, another village north of Stratford. The Ardens were prosperous farmers and Mary must have been a capable girl. When her father died in December

1556, she was responsible for dealing with his will. Two years later at age eighteen, she married John Shakespeare and moved to Stratford, where she had many more responsibilities.

The wife of a sixteenth-century tradesman not only had to care for her husband and children, but she was also expected to run the business when he wasn't there. Mary would have had to know about tanning, preparing leather, and making gloves. She also needed confidence to stand up to her husband's apprentices and employees and the other Stratford tradesmen.

John and Mary Shakespeare's first two children, Joan and Margaret, died as babies. Such early death was not unusual because there was no protection against childhood illnesses. It is remarkable that their next child, William, survived.

William was born when the **plague** was raging in Stratford. That year, nearly fifteen percent of the town's population died of the killer disease.

It is possible that William Shakespeare was born on April 23, 1564. Today, Stratford holds processions and special events on this date. But all that is known for sure is that the Stratford **parish** baptism record reads:

> **1564 April 26 Gulielmus filius Johannes Shakspere**
>
> **(1564 April 26 William son of John Shakspere)**

SHAKESPEARE AT SCHOOL

JOHN SHAKESPEARE'S successful election as a Stratford **burgess** in 1561 allowed him to send his sons, free of charge, to the King's New School, King Edward VI's **grammar school,** in the town. There is no proof, but William probably started at the grammar school at the usual age of six. He would have learned his alphabet, the Lord's Prayer, and perhaps simple arithmetic at the petty, or little school, from the age of four. Some girls were probably also taught at the petty school. They would have been taught sewing rather than writing. But only boys went on to the grammar school.

THE LONG SCHOOL DAY

The school day in the 1500s was long and hard. It began as early as 6 A.M. There was a 2-hour lunch break from 11 A.M. until 1 P.M., and then it ended at 5 P.M. There were eight hours of teaching in a day. The students had a short break for breakfast, and another break in the middle of the afternoon. The day began and ended with prayers.

Shakespeare was taught in this schoolroom located above the Guildhall in Stratford.

This woodcut shows schoolboys at work in an **Elizabethan** schoolroom.

Schoolwork at the grammar schools was based on the study of Latin. Latin had been the language of Ancient Rome, and it was used by statesmen and scholars throughout Europe. Boys read and translated comedies by the Roman dramatists Terence and Plautus, political speeches of Cicero, poems of Ovid, and dialogues by the modern author Erasmus.

One big difference between then and now was that most of the boys' work was spoken out loud. Richard Mulcaster, headmaster of the Merchant Taylors' School in London, believed that the best way to teach boys how to speak, argue, and understand someone else's point of view was by acting out short scenes and dialogues.

When Shakespeare was at the grammar school in Stratford, two of his masters were Thomas Jenkins (between 1575 and 1579) and John Cottom (1579 to about 1582). Jenkins probably had been a pupil of Mulcaster. It is likely that he used his old master's teaching methods. Jenkins may have taught young William to understand how to use words and arguments in lively and dramatic ways.

Jenkins was a **Welshman**. When Shakespeare wrote a comedy called *The Merry Wives of Windsor*—probably in 1597—he included a Welsh schoolmaster. This schoolmaster, named Sir Hugh Evans, asks a boy to recite a Latin lesson. It is a hilarious scene as the boy gets his Latin wrong, and two lively and witty ladies deliberately find rude alternative meanings for the Latin words. The name of the boy in the play is William. This may be a deliberate and fond memory of young Shakespeare's Stratford lessons with his Welsh teacher.

EVANS: *What is your genitive case plural, William?*

WILLIAM: *Genitivo: horum, harum, horum.*

MISTRESS QUICKLY: *Vengeance of Jenny's case! Fie on her! Never name her, child, if she be a whore.*

PAGEANTS AND PROCESSIONS

In the days before movies, television, and radio, when there were no newspapers and less than half the population could read, information and entertainment had to be acted out. Kings, princes, and nobles showed their wealth and power through processions and pageants. These dramatic displays that reenacted a battle or a historical scene were designed to impress their subjects.

THE ROYAL VISIT

In July 1575, Queen Elizabeth I visited Kenilworth Castle, the home of the Earl of Leicester. This was a few miles north of Stratford. The Queen was nearly 42 years old and unmarried. It's now thought that the earl had a plan to persuade the Queen to marry him. He provided three magnificent weeks of entertainment to please and impress her. There were fireworks and plays, hunting and **bearbaiting**. Much of the entertainment took place around the great lake at Kenilworth. The spectacle drew people from miles around. Quite possibly Shakespeare, then an eleven-year-old boy, was among the crowd. He may have seen a play about a battle between the English and the Danes performed by citizens of Coventry. He might also have seen a comic country wedding and a pageant on the lake that was later described like this:

Harry Goldingham was to represent Arion upon the Dolphin's back, but finding his voice to be very hoarse and unpleasant, he tears off his disguise and swears he was none of Arion, not he, but honest Harry Goldingham: which blunt discovery pleased the Queen better than if it had gone through in the right way.

Perhaps it was at Kenilworth that Shakespeare first learned something about actors, which his character, Duke Theseus, puts into words near the end of the play *A Midsummer Night's Dream*.

The best in this kind are but shadows, and the worst are no worse if imagination amend them.

The Church also used processions and plays to show its importance and to present its teachings. Since 1311, a new religious festival called Corpus Christi had been celebrated on a Thursday in June. The celebration quickly came to include another procession. Members of religious organizations and various trade **guilds,** or organizations for craft tradesmen, took part. Eventually this procession developed into a cycle of plays called **mystery plays**. These plays told the history of the world from Adam and Eve to the end of time.

A guild might perform a part of the Christian story that was particularly relevant to its own craft, for example, the carpenters might present the death of Jesus. One feature of these plays was the use of rowdy humor and realistic dialogue. The plays used the everyday lives of the performers and the audience to give the Christian message.

The very last performance of such a cycle of plays in England was given in Coventry, just a few miles from Stratford, in 1580. Shakespeare was sixteen years old at the time. It is possible that he was there in the audience.

All great events were marked by spectacular processions. This procession is from a painting by D. van Asloot, painted in 1615. The painting is in the Victoria and Albert Museum, London. It shows the entry of the Infanta Isabella into the city of Brussels.

MARRIAGE AND FAMILY

When William Shakespeare was 18 years old, he married Anne Hathaway, a woman from Shottery, which was a mile west of Stratford. Anne was about 26 years old.

There are two unusual things about this wedding. For a start, Shakespeare was a very young man. In the 1500s, the average age when men usually married was between 24 and 28. Second, the marriage seems to have been arranged very quickly, because a special license was obtained from the Bishop of Worcester on November 27, 1582. The license allowed William and Anne to marry without the usual three weeks of public notice. This notice, called "publishing the banns," was an announcement in church.

There was a good reason for their speedy marriage. An entry in the Stratford **parish** registers says that "Susanna daughter to William Shakespeare" was baptized on May 26, 1583. Anne must have been three months pregnant when they married.

From the time of their marriage until William bought New Place in Stratford in 1597, Anne and the children probably lived with William's parents on Henley Street. After Susanna, the Shakespeare's had twins, a son Hamnet and a daughter Judith. They were baptized on February 2, 1585.

Shakespeare was baptized and buried in Holy Trinity Church, Stratford, England.

13 Anne daughter to John Shepward

14 John sonne to John Pittes

15 Richard a Bastard of Mr Phillip Moxes servant

21 Thomas sonne to Mr Thomas Raynoldes

31 William sonne to Edward Williams

February 2 Hamnet & Judeth sonne & daughter to william Shakspere

3 Margret daughter to Hugh piggette

10 John sonne to John Ffisher

11 Thomas sonne to Richard Taylor

14 Richard sonne to John Elsome

21 Mary & Jone daughters to John Goodyeare

28 George sonne to George Carles

March 6 Josias sonne to Adrian Young

The baptism of Judith and Hamnet Shakespeare was recorded on February 2, 1585.

A BUSY HOUSEHOLD

William Shakespeare's younger brothers and sisters would almost certainly have been living at the Henley Street house, too, when Anne moved in. Brother Gilbert, a respectable and unmarried tradesman, born in October 1566, died in February 1612. Sister Joan, born in April 1569, outlived all her brothers and sisters. She died in 1646. Another sister, Anne, was born in September 1571 and died in 1579. Almost nothing is known of the brother Richard, except that he was born in March 1574 and died in February 1613. Edmund, the youngest of the brothers and sisters, was born in May 1580.

Following in his brother William's footsteps, Edmund had gone to London to become an actor. He died in 1607 and was buried on December 31, very near to the Globe Theatre in the church of St. Mary Overy—now Southwark Cathedral. The service took place in the morning, presumably so that his fellow actors could attend before their afternoon performance.

THE LOSS OF HIS SON

When Hamnet Shakespeare was born, William was most likely pleased that the Shakespeare family name would continue. But Hamnet died at the age of eleven. He was buried in Stratford on August 11, 1596. There is no record of what his parents thought or felt when they lost their son. The records in the Stratford baptism and burial registers are all that remain to mark his life. The child's name, Hamnet, was not uncommon in Stratford at the time. But it is similar to another name—Hamlet, Prince of Denmark.

The character named Hamlet is the doomed hero of one of Shakespeare's greatest plays. This play was probably written in 1600, just four years after his son's death. In the play, a son sets out to avenge his father's murder. It is perhaps not too unreasonable to suppose that when Shakespeare was writing *Hamlet*, he was painfully aware of the loss of his own son, Hamnet. Hamnet's death marked the end of the Shakespeare family name.

THE UPSTART CROW

THE LOST YEARS

The time between William Shakespeare's marriage to Anne in 1582 and his appearance as a successful young playwright in London in 1592 are sometimes called "the lost years." What was he doing? How did he earn his living? Above all, how did the **grammar** school boy from Stratford get to London and begin working with one of the more famous groups of actors?

One theory is that he became a tutor in the family of a great nobleman. Perhaps it was in the north of England, and perhaps it was on the introduction of his own teacher, John Cottom. From there he may have joined a company of actors, possibly the group called Lord Strange's Men, and traveled with them to London. All of this is possible, but it is not known for sure.

THE QUEEN'S MEN

On the other hand, Shakespeare could have met with a company of actors in Stratford. We know that a number of companies played there when Shakespeare was both a boy and a young man. One of these companies was the Queen's Men. They were paid twenty shillings—about $1.60, a great amount of money in those days—by the Stratford **Corporation** to perform in 1587 when Shakespeare was 23. The Queen's Men was formed in 1583 in an attempt to put the best actors in London under the direct control of Queen Elizabeth I and her council. The company included the famous clowns Richard Tarleton and Robert Wilson, as well as the actors John Bentley and William Knell.

On June 13, 1587, Knell was killed in a duel at Thame in Oxfordshire. It is not known whether the Queen's Men were on their way to Stratford or had already been there, but one thing seems certain: They needed a new actor in a hurry. This may have been when Shakespeare got his first job.

This woodcut shows Robert Greene, the writer who called Shakespeare an "upstart crow."

It is very likely that the first play Shakespeare wrote was the comedy *Two Gentlemen of Verona*. In that play, the character of Launce would have been played by the company's clown. Launce has a dog, Crab, and there is a very funny scene between the two of them. It is known that Richard Tarleton had a dog, and that he sometimes had "conversations" with it as part of his act. Did Shakespeare write his first comic role for this master comedian and his dog? If he did, it would have been one of Tarleton's last roles, because he died in 1588. After that time, there are no more dogs in Shakespeare's plays.

The Queen's Men also performed the plays of Robert Greene, who provides another unusual piece of evidence. The evidence suggests that Shakespeare was well-known in London by 1592. In that year, Greene wrote a sarcastic attack about a new, young writer.

. . . an upstart crow, beautified with our feathers, that with his Tiger's heart wrapped in a player's hide . . . is in his own conceit the only Shake-scene in a country.

This joke, using Shakespeare's name, is also being sarcastic about his ability to write plays.

Greene, who was educated at the university, is attacking a grammar school boy for daring to compete as a playwright. Was Greene's work no longer popular? Had Shakespeare's plays begun to replace his in the **repertoire** of the Queen's Men?

The "Ely Palace" portrait, is said to be of William Shakespeare.

Whatever the reason, by 1592, William Shakespeare was successful enough to be attacked by other writers. Within two years, he had enough money to buy himself a **share** in the Chamberlain's Men, which was the company of actors with whom he would work for the rest of his life.

THE PLAGUE, POEMS, AND PATRONS

By the early 1590s, Shakespeare had established himself as a playwright. But his career was interrupted by that terrifying and unpredictable fact of **Elizabethan** life—the bubonic **plague**. This terrible disease was spread by fleas living on rats. The rats thrived in the filthy living conditions of London and other cities.

The Thames River was an open sewer. People dumped their rubbish in the narrow streets. Anyone infected by the plague was isolated and left to die. The front doors of victims' houses were marked with a red cross. The red marks, the cries of the dying, and the creak of carts carrying bodies to the burial pits were the dreadful sights and sounds of the time.

TOURING COMPANIES

There was a violent outbreak of the plague in 1592–1593. Public meetings "at plays, **bearbaitings**, bowlings, and other like assemblies" were banned. Acting companies had to apply for licenses to perform outside London. The actors may have carried the disease with them. Surely, neither players nor audiences in country towns would have had much enthusiasm for entertainment.

At this time, Shakespeare was probably a member of a touring company. He was also developing another kind of work. He was writing poems and arranging for them to be printed. Publishing poetry would earn him money and, perhaps, attract the support of a wealthy **patron**, who might provide other opportunities.

This woodcut of the plague in London shows how terrified people were of catching it.

FLATTERING HIS PATRON

In Shakespeare's time, any book that was printed was entered on a list known as the Stationers' Register. On April 18, 1593, Shakespeare's poem *Venus and Adonis* was entered into the register by the poem's printer, Richard Field. Field was a Stratford man who, like the poet, had made a successful move to London. *The Rape of Lucrece* was registered on May 9, 1594 by another printer, John Harrison. Both poems were dedicated to a young nobleman, HENRY WRIOTHESLEY, EARL OF SOUTHAMPTON. The earl was rich, dashing, and influential. Shakespeare tried hard to win the earl's patronage. Getting a patron meant gaining financial support, protection, and an influential friend. All of these things were much needed in such unpredictable times. Shakespeare's dedications to the young earl follow the fashion of the time. They exaggerate his high position, making the poet very humble. Shakespeare wrote

> *. . . only if your honor seem but pleased, I account myself highly praised . . .*

He goes on to promise that if the earl likes the first poem, then something more serious will follow.

Venus and Adonis is an elegant and witty story based on a poem by Ovid, one of the Roman poets Shakespeare studied at school. Shakespeare did not make a simple translation, but instead rewrote Ovid. He shows Venus, the goddess of love, chasing a bashful and inexperienced young man. The young man finally escapes her advances to go hunting. It is both comic and sexy and was an immediate bestseller.

The Rape of Lucrece, also based on a story in Ovid, is more complex and serious. With these poems, Shakespeare established his reputation as a versatile poet. He began to attract the fashionable and aristocratic support he needed. This helped him financially and helped to make him successful.

This painting, by John de Critz the Elder in 1603, is of Henry Wriothesley, 3rd Earl of Southampton and patron of Shakespeare.

AT HOME IN LONDON

In October 1596, William Shakespeare was living in St. Helen's **parish** in the City of London. Today, the area is bounded by Bishopsgate Street, Houndsditch, and Leadenhall Street, and is a little way north of the Tower of London. In 1597, Shakespeare was listed as one of those from that parish who owed 5 **shillings**, or about 40 cents, in unpaid tax. By 1600, when he still owed 13 shillings and 4 pence, or $1.10, the matter was referred to the Bishop of Winchester. The bishop was responsible for the "Liberty of the Clink" area on the south bank of the Thames River. This was where the Globe Theatre had been built in early 1599. This bishop's involvement suggests that Shakespeare had now moved across the river to Southwark to be nearer the new theater. He seems to have settled his tax debts, because his name disappears from the lists by 1601.

SUCCESS

Shakespeare was a successful actor, poet, and playwright, and he had a **share** in the profits of the Chamberlain's Men. Back in Stratford, his father's situation was improving, perhaps with help from William's own moneymaking ventures. Within a year, the glover's son, who had left his home town to seek his fortune in London, was able to buy Stratford's second largest house. It was called New Place. Shakespeare's wife and daughters moved in.

Shakespeare had learned his trades of writing and acting. Now he was in a position to profit from it.

A map of London at the end of the 1500s shows the theater locations.

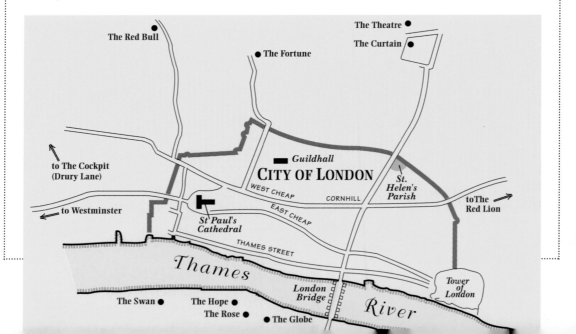

New Playhouses

In 1572, an "Acte for the punishment of Vagabondes,"or people without a permanent home, made it necessary for traveling actors to find the patronage of a powerful nobleman. A nobleman could protect them from possible arrest. A company led by James Burbage, a former carpenter, had been adopted by the Earl of Leicester. In 1576, Burbage leased part of the site of the old Holywell Priory, just north of the City of London. It was on the corner of what is now Curtain Road and New Inn Yard. There Burbage built a permanent theater for his company and other companies visiting London.

The Theatre, as it was called, was the second playhouse building in London. The first, the Red Lion, was built in 1567 by Burbage's brother-in-law, John Brayne. Within a year of the completion of the Theatre, another playhouse, the Curtain, was built almost next door on the south side of what is now Holywell Lane. When Shakespeare was in London, he would have walked to one of these playhouses most days. However, in the summer of 1599, the Chamberlain's Men moved across the river to the Globe.

A sketch of London Bridge in 1627 by Claude de Jongh shows the Globe and Hope Theatres on the far right.

The Excitement of the City

London by **Elizabethan** standards was a huge city of more than 200,000 people. They were crammed into narrow streets and dark alleyways that were criss-crossed by ditches and drains. It was a dangerous city of thieves, prostitutes, spies, and tricksters. It was a city of enormous contrasts. It had the great wealth of nobility, royalty, and rich merchants, and it had utter poverty and degradation. It was a place of tremendous energy, where life could be lived to the fullest. But life also could be snuffed out at any moment by murder or disease.

London was Shakespeare's second home. But unlike some of his fellow writers, for example, Ben Jonson or Thomas Dekker, Shakespeare didn't write much about London. His plays inhabit countries of the mind. He asked his audiences to imagine France or Italy or a rural English Warwickshire recreated in a loving dream. If he did love London, he seems to have loved Stratford even more.

THE CHAMBERLAIN'S MEN

SHAKESPEARE THE SHAREHOLDER

By the autumn of 1594, the worst of the **plague** was over for a time. Normal life began again. The **Lord Chamberlain** asked the Lord Mayor of London to allow his company of actors to perform at the Cross Keys Inn on Gracechurch Street, which is near the present day monument to the Great Fire of London. In December, the company played twice at the royal palace at Greenwich as part of the Queen's Christmas entertainment. The royal household accounts name three men who were paid for the company's performances. They were William Kemp, Richard Burbage, and William Shakespeare. They were described as "servants to the Lord Chamberlain." By the end of 1594, when Shakespeare was 30 years old, the company of actors with which he was now working was securely established as the Chamberlain's Men.

The group of men who worked together were experienced actors. Unlike previous companies, the Chamberlain's Men enjoyed many years of stability and success with few people joining or leaving. Shakespeare was one of those who bought a **share** in the company.

He invested money, perhaps funds from the sale of his poems to the printers or a gift from his **patron**, the Earl of Southampton. In return, he received a share in the company's profits. He worked hard as shareholder, actor, and playwright to achieve success for the company.

The Chamberlain's Men performed plays by many writers, but their special connection with Shakespeare was unusual for the time. He was the first resident playwright in London; that is, he was employed to write especially for the company.

This 1591 portrait of Lord Chamberlain Hunsdon hangs in the National Portrait Gallery in London.

This title page is from Ben Jonson's play *Every Man in His Humour* in which Shakespeare acted.

SHAKESPEARE, COMPANY PLAYWRIGHT

Shakespeare wrote many different types of plays for the company. He had made his mark as a writer of plays about English history, but he also developed the type of play known as a comedy. Shakespeare's comedies are not simply funny, although they often are very amusing. The word *comedy* means that the play ends on a mainly hopeful note and reflects a positive view of life. Comedies are love stories and are often complicated by misunderstandings that can be humorous or serious. The comedies of Shakespeare show the confusion and suffering that people can feel and cause in others. His comedies also show kindness, wit, and high spirits. It is this wide range of human experience, and of types of characters that make these plays so attractive.

Shakespeare had the popular comic actor Will Kemp in the company. Shakespeare made the most of Kemp's ability to entertain an audience. It is likely that Kemp first played the character Bottom in *A Midsummer Night's Dream*. Bottom is taken away by the Queen of the Fairies, treated like a king, given every luxury, and then left alone. He wonders if it was all a dream. The role of Bottom would have used Kemp's larger-than-life personality with great success.

EVERY MAN IN
his Humor.

As it hath beene sundry times
publickly acted by the right
Honorable the Lord Cham-
berlaine his seruants.

Written by BEN. IOHNSON.

Quod non dant proceres, dabit Histrio.

Haud tamen inuidias vati, quem pulpita pascunt.

Imprinted at London for *Walter Burre*, and are to
be sould at his shoppe in *Paules Church-yarde.*
1601.

It may be difficult now to imagine boy actors, whose voices had not yet changed, playing Shakespeare's female characters. The heroines of the comedies are usually very attractive, warm-hearted, quick-witted young women who run rings around the men. Twists in the stories often put them into situations where they disguise themselves as boys. Such confusion is the stuff of Shakespeare's comedies.

THE GLOBE THEATRE

THE BURBAGE FAMILY

James Burbage and his sons, Richard and Cuthbert, played an important part in Shakespeare's life. As a boy, Shakespeare would probably have seen James act with the Earl of Leicester's Men in Stratford. James built the Theatre, where many of Shakespeare's plays were first seen.

The Chamberlain's Men and its playwright were doing well at the Theatre. Francis Meres, a young student, enjoyed going to plays. He wrote about them admiringly in 1598.

As Plautus and Seneca are accounted the best for comedy and tragedy among the Latins, so Shakespeare among the English is most excellent in both kinds for the stage.

It would have been a blow to the company when they learned that the lease on the land where the Theatre was built was not going to be renewed. Now the Theatre would have to be demolished. Where would they perform? The Burbages were not men to be easily discouraged. They painstakingly dismantled the Theatre, plank by plank, and used its timbers to build a magnificent large new playhouse on the south bank of the Thames River.

They called the new theater the Globe, and it opened in 1599. It was expensive to build, and the Burbages could raise only 50 percent of the cost themselves. Five of the shareholders in the company of the Chamberlain's Men, including Shakespeare, put up 10 percent each to make up the total sum. Shakespeare had evidently earned well in the 1590s. As a shareholder in the Globe, he was in line to receive greater profits than before. He was not only a successful man in the theater, but in business, too.

Shakespeare and Richard Burbage worked together as business partners and as artists for at least twenty years. Burbage was the leading actor who first played many of Shakespeare's most demanding roles. His roles included the leads in the plays *Hamlet, Othello,* and *King Lear.* These plays are called tragedies. They explore suffering and the clash between good and evil, hope and despair, love and conflict. They make huge demands on the actor's emotions and understanding. Shakespeare must have been very confident of Burbage's ability. It is likely, too, that the actor's comments and questions affected the script that was eventually performed. Even today's playwrights often adjust their plays during rehearsal.

But it wasn't all tragedy on the stage of the Globe. Shakespeare's comedies, English history plays, and accounts of the leaders of Ancient Greece and Rome were all popular. In his plays, Shakespeare raised questions about the qualities needed in a good king and the rights and wrongs of opposing a bad or weak ruler. Such questions might have been explored on stage using all the glamor of the past, but in **Elizabethan** London, they were real and urgent questions.

The questions were no less relevant when the new king, James I, came to the throne in 1603. The Chamberlain's Men, renamed the King's Men, had a special role to play in performing before the **Court**. Their plays would have been the subject of intense debate.

In the outdoor theaters, audiences were large, noisy, and enthusiastic, but no less responsive and critical. Even foreign visitors found the theater one of the most exciting elements of city life, as many people still do today.

This drawing of the Globe Theatre is based on Cornelius de Visscher's view of London in 1616.

The Globe

DANGEROUS TIMES

Acting companies lived on the fringes of **court** life. As intelligent, literate men of the world, they were easily caught up in the political and diplomatic intrigues of the reigns of Queen Elizabeth and King James. They also had freedom of movement when they toured throughout England and on the mainland of Europe. Above all, plays were an important source of information and propaganda. They were a way to influence opinion. There was always the danger that performances might cause a disturbance.

Actors and playwrights might be available to act as spies or secret messengers. But even though they could be used by the politicians, they still had to be controlled.

An example of the way actors and writers got involved in politics can be seen in the career of Christopher Marlowe. He was a university man, a poet, and a writer of plays. In the 1580s and 1590s, he wrote *Doctor Faustus*, *Tamburlaine the Great,* and *The Jew of Malta.*

Marlowe died mysteriously in a tavern fight at Deptford on May 30, 1593. The story was that it was simply the result of an argument about the bill. But recent research discovered many more facts. It seems that Marlowe was almost certainly involved in some spying activity and that he was killed because he was getting in the way of the political ambitions of the Earl of Essex.

Sir Francis Walsingham was Queen Elizabeth's spymaster. This portrait in the National Portrait Gallery is said to be by John de Critz the Elder, in about 1585.

The Chamberlain's Men were involved with the Earl of Essex a few years later. By 1601, the Earl was becoming desperate in his attempts to be the Queen's favorite and her husband. He made his move on February 7, 1601, by threatening a **rebellion**. He failed and was executed three weeks later. The day before the rebellion started, the plotters had gone to the Globe Theatre. They attended a specially arranged performance of Shakespeare's *Richard II,* a play about rebellion and the killing of a king. The Chamberlain's Men managed to avoid any punishment for their innocent involvement in Essex's activities. They even performed at Court again on February 24, the night before the earl's execution. But there must have been some anxious moments as the rebellion investigation proceeded.

THE STATE CENSOR

Whenever a company wished to put on a new play, it had to send its **text** to an official of the court. This was the **Lord Chamberlain,** who, with his assistant, the **Master of the Revels**, was responsible for all public performances. They often rejected plays, demanded cuts in the text, or insisted that scenes be rewritten. In 1605, a play called *Eastward Ho!,* written by Ben Jonson, George Chapman, and John Marston, was performed. But a few lines that seemed to insult the Scots gave offense to King James who was Scottish. The authors were imprisoned and only released when influential friends spoke on their behalf.

Some years earlier, probably in 1592 or 1593, a group of writers began a play about a famous Englishman who lived during the time of King Henry VIII. This Englishman was Sir Thomas More. When the play landed on the desk of Sir Edward Tilney, Master of the Revels, he was unhappy that one of its themes was an attack on foreigners living in London. This was currently a source of tension in London. Tilney demanded rewrites. It looks as though Shakespeare was called in, perhaps as much as ten years later, to help. But Tilney still had objections, and the play was never performed.

Ben Jonson, actor and playwright, once killed a man and was later put in prison for his part in writing a play that offended King James I.

A SUCCESSFUL BUSINESSMAN

It is easy to see William Shakespeare as only a great playwright and a genius in his use of the English language. He was both of these. But he was also a clever and hardheaded businessman. He was committed to making money for himself and his family. His father was a master glover, a merchant, a property owner, a dealer in raw materials, and a significant figure in the running of his home town of Stratford-upon-Avon. William Shakespeare was a man of trade, too. His craft was words. His skill lay in the new world of the London theater. But like his father, he seems to have used his wealth in a variety of ways. One thing that made William determined to be successful was quite possibly a wish to restore the good name of the Shakespeare family in Stratford. It had declined with his father's decline in fortune.

NEW PLACE

William Shakespeare bought New Place in Stratford on May 4, 1597, for £60 in silver, or about $100. It was the second biggest house in Stratford and was built at the end of the 1400s by Sir Hugh Clopton, another Stratford man who had prospered in London. Shakespeare's wife and family moved into New Place. By the time Shakespeare began to spend most of his time in Stratford, around 1610, they had acquired other property in the town. This included 107 acres of land at Welcombe.

It is thought that William and Anne had an unhappy marriage, but to judge from his prosperity throughout these years, she must have been a good business partner, like her mother-in-law, Mary. Shakespeare's eldest daughter, Susanna, was married in 1607 to a doctor, John Hall. They lived at New Place with her parents after the marriage. They had a daughter, Elizabeth, who was born in 1608 and lived until 1670. Elizabeth was the last direct relative of William Shakespeare.

This early drawing is of New Place, Stratford, that Shakespeare bought in 1597.

William Shakespeare,
the "Flower Portrait."

Throughout his time in London, William Shakespeare continued his links with Stratford. In 1598, a neighbor from home, Richard Quiney, seems to have persuaded William to lend him some money. Quiney and his partner needed help with a business idea. Similarly, once he moved back to Stratford, he continued his links with London. The King's Men needed his business sense, as well as his playwriting skills.

THE GLOBE BURNS DOWN

In March 1613, Shakespeare bought some property in London. He bought part of the gatehouse of the Blackfriars Theatre on the north bank of the Thames River. This was not far from his company's indoor theater. But disaster struck on June 29 of that same year. During a performance of the play *Henry VIII,* which was probably written by Shakespeare with the younger writer John Fletcher, the **thatched** roof of the theater was accidentally set on fire. The Globe burned down. Within a year it was rebuilt, but it had a new resident playwright, John Fletcher. William Shakespeare seems to have written nothing more for his theater.

WILL AND DEATH

O n July 6, 1614, a great fire swept through the narrow streets and wooden houses of Stratford. It was a devastating blow to many families. It caused much loss of property, livelihood, and prosperity. Although New Place was not damaged, the Shakespeares must have felt the effects on the town's slumping economy.

ENCLOSURE

In an attempt to make up their losses, some Stratford landowners decided to follow a national trend. They would make changes to the way they farmed their land. This change was called enclosure. It meant that large landowners evicted tenants from their property and turned the land over to cheaper types of farming. The result was widespread poverty and unemployment for the small tenant farmers, but increased profits for the landowners.

In Stratford, a group led by Thomas Combe, Arthur Mainwaring, and William Replingham was in favor of enclosure. Another group, led by a lawyer Thomas Greene opposed them. It is not clear which side Shakespeare was on.

The final page of Shakespeare's will of 1616 has his signature.

As a landowner, Shakespeare would have had much to gain. But he also seems to have concluded that the supporters of enclosure would never get their plan off the ground. He was right. In spite of bullying tactics by Thomas Combe and some tricky negotiating by Replingham, the enclosure proposals were defeated in a court of law. But that did not happen until 1619. By then Shakespeare had been dead for three years.

PROVIDING FOR HIS FAMILY

In the middle of this bitter disagreement, which caused much anger and distress in Stratford, Shakespeare wrote his will. This was in January 1616. The next month his daughter, Judith, was married. She was 31. Judith married Thomas Quiney, a Stratford wine merchant. In January, William's will included a bequest of £100 or about $160, to Thomas. But Thomas did not turn out too well. Judith was pregnant when they married. In March, another woman claimed to be having Thomas' baby, too. She and the child died in childbirth that month, and Thomas was punished by the Church for his offense. William Shakespeare rewrote his will to exclude Quiney. Only Judith inherited the £100 and a few other things, including "a broad silver and gilt bowl."

Even though she was provided for, Judith's share was much less than that of her elder sister Susanna and her husband, Dr. John Hall. They inherited New Place, the other properties, and most of the contents of the houses. This most likely included Shakespeare's books, too. Shakespeare's sister, Joan, received £20, or about $32, and his clothes. Her sons each received £5 or about $8.

Other friends and relatives received small gifts. But the best-known **bequest** went to his wife, Anne. She was to have "the second-best bed." People have often taken this as a sign that William and Anne did not get along, but there is no reason to think that. Since a widow usually remained in her own home after the death of her husband, no special arrangement in a will was needed. Since the best bed was reserved for guests, the "second-best bed" was the one she had slept in all her married life.

These arrangements of the will were made just in time. On April 23, 1616, William Shakespeare died at home in Stratford. He was exactly 52 years old.

This is the monument to Shakespeare in Holy Trinity Church, Stratford.

FAME AND THE FIRST FOLIO

Shakespeare also left small sums of money to his actor friends, Richard Burbage, John Hemmings, and Henry Condell. They were to buy rings to remember the man who had helped them achieve fame and fortune on the stage. They repaid his friendly gesture by an act that was to guarantee that Shakespeare's reputation would live on. They arranged for the printing of a collected edition of his plays.

THE FIRST COLLECTION OF PLAYS

The First Folio, published in 1623, contains 36 of the 37 plays generally agreed to have been written by Shakespeare. Eighteen of these plays had not been printed before. The others had appeared earlier as individual **texts** known as Quartos. Folio and Quarto refer to the size of the paper used by the printers. A copy of a new First Folio would have cost £1, or around $1.60 in 1623. This was equivalent to a month's wages for a skilled worker. It came without a book cover, so there would be more cost to have a leather binding. If one of the 250 copies surviving today were to be sold, it would sell for about $1,600,000.

Richard Burbage died in 1619. This left Hemmings and Condell to sort out the playscripts. They had several possible sources. One was **prompt book** copies of the whole plays that would have been used at the Globe or the Blackfriars theaters. These may even have been Shakespeare's own original copies. Another source was the actors' individual parts written out on long scrolls of paper. A final source would be earlier printed versions.

Some of the plays had been performed regularly for many years, others were nearly forgotten. In bringing them all together in one large book, Hemmings and Condell were celebrating a brilliant man of the theater. They were also making sure that the King's Men would continue to profit from Shakespeare's genius.

William Shakespeare was buried in the parish church in Stratford. A monument to him has this famous inscription:

Reader, for Jesus' Sake forbear

To dig the dust enclosed here:

*Blessed be he
that spares these Stones,*

*And cursed be he
that moves my bones.*

A statue of Shakespeare holds a quill pen, the symbol of his art and craft and a symbol of his profession. It was the way he made his money, restored his father's good name, and supported his wife and family.

At the beginning of the First Folio, poems and letters from a number of Shakespeare's admirers tried to say something about his genius. One of his fellow playwrights, Ben Jonson, who had published his own *Collected Works* in 1616, understood better than most that Shakespeare's life and work could never be separated from the need to survive and prosper in the often dangerous and always insecure world of the theater. Jonson recognized that Shakespeare was more than just a man of his time. In his poem in the First Folio, Jonson wrote,

> *Thou art a Monument,*
> *without a tomb,*
>
> *And art alive still,*
> *while thy Booke doth live,*
>
> *And we have wits to read,*
> *and praise to give . . .*

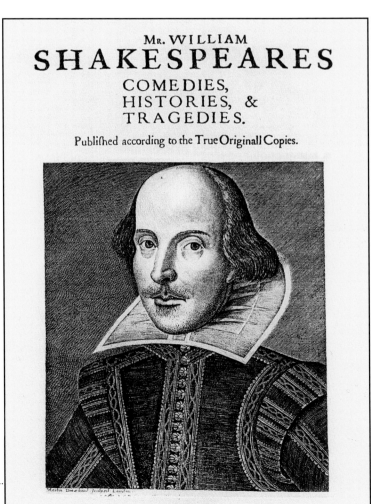

Shakespeare appears on the **frontispiece** of the First Folio.

GLOSSARY

bearbaiting sport in which dogs fight a chained bear

bequest something given after death, especially money or property

burgess citizen of a town, usually having special responsibilities

corporation town whose rules of government place responsibility on a group of elected members to act together

court family, household, or followers of a king, queen, or member of the royal family

Elizabethan relating to Queen Elizabeth I of England and her reign, from 1533–1603

frontispiece illustration facing the title page of a book

grammar school originally a school for teaching the elements of grammar, especially Latin grammar

guild association of merchants or persons in a particular trade or craft

Lord Chamberlain royal official responsible for the Court's entertainment

Master of the Revels official in the Lord Chamberlain's office who has special responsibility for court entertainment

mystery plays collection of religious plays performed at the festival of Corpus Christi

parish district that has its own church and clergymen

patron nobleman who supported, often financially, the work of poets, artists, musicians, or playing companies

plague also known as the bubonic plague—a highly infectious disease transmitted by fleas that live on rats

player actor

playhouse theater

prompt book book of the play that is used by a person who tells the actors what to say when they forget

rebellion fight against one's government

repertoire list of plays that an acting company is prepared to perform

share agreement that allows a person to receive a percentage of the profits from performances

shilling coin worth one-twentieth of an English pound sterling, having about eight cents in value

text original words of a writer

thatch straw used as a roof

Welshman man from the country of Wales

MORE BOOKS TO READ

Aliki. *William Shakespeare & the Globe.* New York: HarperCollins Children's Books, 1999.

Claybourne, Anna and Rebecca Treays. *World of Shakespeare.* Tulsa, Okla.: E D C Publishing, 1997.

Ganeri, Anita. *Young Person's Guide to Shakespeare.* San Diego, Calif.: Harcourt, 1999.

Morley, Jacqueline. *Shakespeare's Theater.* Lincolnwood, Ill.: NTC Contemporary Publishing Company, 1994.

Stanley, Diane. *The Bard of Avon.* New York: Morrow, William & Company, Incorporated, 1998.

ADDITIONAL RESOURCES

African-American Shakespeare Company
5214-F Diamond Heights Blvd.
PMB 923
San Francisco, CA 94131
Tel: (415) 333-1918
This company's mission is to produce European classical works with an African-American cultural perspective

The Shakespeare Theatre
516 8th Street SE
Washington, DC 20003
(202) 547-3230
One of the top Shakespeare companies in the U.S., its mission is to produce and preserve classical theater and to develop new audiences for classical theater.

INDEX